HIGH MAGICK 101
A BEGINNER'S GUIDE TO HIGH MAGICK

High Magick 101

A Beginner's Guide to High Magick

David Thompson

To my Patron Gods, Hermes and Aphrodite

Disclaimer

First:

A Legal Disclaimer:

By Law, I am obliged to let you know that this is for entertainment purposes only, and does not claim to prevent or cure any diseases. The advice in this book should not be construed as financial, medical, or psychological advice. Please seek such advice from a professional.

By purchasing this book, and by engaging with the teachers and other students, or by viewing the video from this course, and by reading the course handouts, you understand that results are not guaranteed. In light of this and in the unlikely event that this course does not work for you or, in the very unlikely event, this book causes physical harm to you or a loved one, you agree that you will not hold David Thompson, our affiliates and employees liable for any damages you may experience or incur.

Each individual's success depends on his or her background, dedication, desire, and motivation.

Warning

A Warning:

This is very powerful material. When worked properly, you may see unexpected results. These rituals and petitions are like electricity, the energy will flow in the direction of the intended output. In saying this, please be firm in your intentions and make absolutely sure what you want is truly want you desire.

As they say, be careful what you wish for, you just might get it.

Introduction

High Magick 101, The Beginner's Guide to High Magick is a conversion of my popular online course of the same name.

This book is intended to guide the neophyte magician from zero knowledge up to becoming an accomplished magician.

Lofty goals. But I've seen my students go from have literally zero knowledge, just a burning desire to work magick, to where they are doing amazing work, utilizing gods such as Apollo and Poseidon.

I do have to say this, one of my original students took this class, at the time her son was in the hospital with a rare lung disease. No, the magick did not spontaneously cure the boy, but a ritual to Apollo did cause a set of donor lungs to become available. Within 12 hours of her ritual to Apollo her son was in the operating room, being saved.

This is because magick works through US. Pray all you want to any deity, but the miracles occur by placing you in the right spot at the right time.

You won't become rich overnight, but magick will tilt the playing field in your favor. Your resume will be viewed with preference, your ads for your business will be highly effective.

With all magick, you have to meet the power half-way, by honing your abilities in your career, making yourself available to meet that possible soul-mate, etc.

I have, a few times, manifested cash using magick. I did a silent ritual to Bune (Daemon of wealth) and in a few hours I was walking along a busy street in Los Angeles, and I saw an old, dusty wallet. I picked it up and inspected it. No ID. And $200.00 in cash inside. But no clue as to who might have lost it. I did a silent "thank you" to Bune. He put me in the right spot to find this wallet. (Rest assured, if the wallet HAD contained ID, I would have tracked the owner down... but no ID, no way to find the guy who lost it).

Inside this book, you will find advice on what tools and items you'll likely need. I'll break down what you REALLY need for High Magick, as well as instructions on how to cast a circle, petition a deity, WHO to petition, when to work the ritual, and possible offerings.

I also take you through the steps necessary to incorporate Chaos Magick, Sigils, Planetary Magick Squares, and the use of Angels and Saints in your rituals. I have a chapter on troubleshooting non-working magick, the use of a pendulum and Tarot Cards in finding out why some magick tends to fail.

Along with reference tables for when to work what type of magick, colors to use for specific magick (love, money, etc.), what days of the week are best for what type of magick.

There is also a companion workbook, larger in size, designed to be a journal that you can log each ritual as you work it, with spaces to record the date & time, which God/Goddess/Being you summoned, the details of the ritual, and eventual outcome. This is a necessary part of working magick: tracking and keeping notes to see what does, and doesn't work. This will become your journal for your own magick, a Grimoire.

Grimoires that magicians have used for centuries all started out as diaries written by the practitioners of magick, often kept in secret, written in a secret language only known by the magician. This was because the authorities at the time took a dim view of any magic workings. Thankfully, we live in a more enlightened time right now.

David Thompson

2

High Magick defined

What is "High Magick?"

There are many different definitions of this type of magick, and we'll be working with my own.

This is the Magick of Ascension, which brings to you unique tools by which you can manifest what you desire into reality on the physical plain by using the power and energy of other beings, beings we sometimes refer to as "Gods and Goddesses".

This is the magick I have worked since I was a teenager, taking parts from one book on spells, some from another book about ancient magick, and some from books about esoteric magick once practiced in ancient cultures, such as Babylon.

I have had people get after me for also including Daemons

in my magick, often worried somehow and in some way my soul will be lost. Some teachers online seem to believe that only their methods will produce results, but in this magick of mine, I get staggering results.

Yes, High Magick can also utilize so-called "Daemons", but that is beyond the scope of this particular book. I am presenting material for the beginner, someone who wishes to "dabble" into the arts and science of Magick. Daemonology isn't for the dabbler! You can reach out to me via my Facebook page or one of my groups if you wish to look into this aspect of High Magick.

It's a smoosh-up ("Smoosh" is a word. Go ahead, look it up on Webster's, I'll wait...) of multiple magical disciplines, such as Enochian, Wiccan, Ceremonial, and a hint of a few others just to spice things up.

It's my own system. I make use of deities, a few props, and a lot of altered mental states.

In my other books, I typically give the reader a list of rituals to work, but with this book, I give you the tools to work up your own rituals. This isn't a magick cookbook, so much as it's a

I have also thrown in Sigil Magick as well. This where I will guide you through the various methods for generating a symbol known as a "Sigil" which is an abstract representation of your desire. I work two differing methods of creating a sigil from a statement of desire. I'll go over both of these two techniques in detail later on in this book.

I have the ability to sense and hear spirits. A lot of what I'll be presenting was given to me by one of several beings I have worked with in the past: Apollo, Hermes, Aphrodite, Lilith, Bune, Belial, Lucifer, and Ba'al.

Don't worry, I'll not be asking you to work with any specific being. I will gently guide you in the right direction to the safest Gods or Goddesses I can suggest.

This is why you will not need a "circle of protection", and why I'll be teaching you a method of casting a circle that will facilitate communication with Gods/Goddesses and what I call "Benign Entities."

You will be guided through the process of choosing a God/Goddess or other Entity.

Then you will be taught the best ways to call upon this Entity with will increase the possibility that the Entity will join with you to help you achieve your goals and manifestations.

3

Ritual Items for High Magick

Items used for high Magick

When working High Magick, a magician typically tries to represent all the elements of the Earth in the circle. The tools I present in this chapter have their place, representing Earth, Fire, Water, and Air.

The Altar

This is the heart of any magick practice. Make sure you choose a table large enough to function and not so big it takes over the space, making it hard to get around.

Temporary altars are very commonplace, as you may not have room for a permanent altar. I used a card table for years before I created a specific spot for a more permanent altar.

Make sure, if using a temporary altar, to store your materials in a safe place to avoid anyone else poking through the items. Outside energy can have a negative effect on your magick items. Someone pawing through your candles or crystals can cause a large enough shift in the energy to cause a ritual to fail.

Altar Cloth

For the longest time, I simply used a old towel as an altar cloth. I had two from when I was a kid, both thin. One was green, the other was red. I used these versus buying a special purpose altar cloth.

It's not needed, and only serves as decoration for your rituals.

I find I tend to spill wax on any cloth I use, so when I purchased an altar cloth I looked for the least expensive one on Amazon. Triple Goddess With Pentagram - 24" x 24", black with gold. It's served me quite well for the last 4 years.

Incense

Incense represents the element AIR.

Most any type of incense can be used in magick.

Some beings will prefer a specific incense while others don't appear to really have a preference.

Personally, I burn an incense charcoal in a brass burner with a screen. Then I will place the incense on the charcoal.

I will use a base of Frankincense resin, of a high grade. Avoid the less expensive grades as they often may not be actual Frankincense. Try to find "Organic" and products labeled as "Frankincense Tears", as they're usually the best quality.

If you are using a stick form of incense, make sure to test a piece before using it in an enclosed space, as many are highly perfumed and can trigger allergies.

It's also quite useful to sanctify your space. If you use a temporary altar, then you need to use Frankincense to purify and sanctify your space prior to working at ritual. It's difficult to attract any spirit into your space if the energies are chaotic or negative.

What I do, I start the charcoal and once it's fully ashed over, I'll place a sizable chunk of Frankincense on the charcoal. I'll allow the smoke to fill my space. Only then do I start my workings and begin adding the incense for the particular ritual I am working.

Once I have the particular deity summoned, they will often begin to affect the incense smoke. I have had them cause the smoke to twist and curl, and often forming faces in the smoke itself.

My website has a gallery of images of this happening.

If you cannot use incense, you can use essential oils in a diffuser to partially achieve the same effects as smoking incense, and is recommended for times when a co-inhabitant of your dwelling is sensitive to the smoke of the incense.

Athame

Many people love to use various ceremonial daggers when practicing magick.

The Athame is typically a black handled dagger, primary used to direct energy during a ceremony. Many people tend to collect various types.

I have used one, but I have found my finger is just as good for this, and is a heck of a lot cheaper.

One can also use a quartz wand instead of a traditional Athame. This would avoid awkward questions from anyone who happens across your magical tool stash. The additional plus of using a crystal wand is that it'll magnify your energy and direct it quite accurately.

This is one of the tools that isn't a must have. It's cool to have it, tho.

If you use an Athame, don't get too stabby with it.

Candles

A candle represents the element "Fire" on your altar.

Of all the items used in High Magick, the candle is the one thing you should always try to use. Candles do not need to be expensive or elaborate.

For my basic altar set-up, I will use four candles. Two white and two black, as this encompasses the full range of all colors.

Then I will add a 5th candle in a color which corresponds to the magick I am performing. In the appendix, I have a list of colors and what they represent.

For my altar candles, I use a 3" pillar candle. The white ones I get from the local department store, as it's easy to find white. I suggest at least the 3" tall candles, but I often use the 6" tall candles on my altar.

On Amazon, I buy the black candles found by searching "Megacandles 3-inch candle" as their quality is excellent and the price is quite good.

You do not need more than ONE altar candle, but go with white if all you want is a single candle. White will stand-in for most any type of color for most magick.

If you live in a house or apartment and have to share your space, it is fine to use "fake" candles. I'd recommend those

LED tea lights.

Crystals

Crystals can represent the element "Earth" on your altar.

This is where a lot of magicians and other people tend to put most of their energy. Mine is incense, frankly, and other people love to collect crystals. Entire books are written about crystals in magick. I'll not even try to compete with those useful books.

Instead, I'll simply suggest you look into the more useful crystals that can be used in magick.

Quartz: I have found that small five to six inch "points" are very useful to have on my altar. If you have more than one, place one on each edge of the altar, to assist in channeling the energy through the area.

I have a large point I use instead of an Athame. Plus, it keeps away the negative energies that can be attached to your space.

After a while and definitely before use, you need to cleanse the crystals.

Not all crystals can withstand immersion in water, and some are even damaged by direct sunlight. I personally use salt to reset my crystals. I will place the crystal into a small bowl, and cover it with coarse canning or pickling salt. (This is also my preferred salt for use in cooking and making barbecue seasonings)

Leave the crystal in the salt for about 24-48 hours. The dispose of the salt in a safe manner. Don't go scattering the used salt on your lawn or garden, as salt can retard the growth of plants. (In ancient times, the invading armies would burn the village's crops and spread salt on the ground, so they can't grow anything anymore)

Then, after the crystal is cleansed, I take them into my space and simple pass them through incense smoke. Easy.

A Chalice or Goblet

A chalice serves two purposes on your altar. They can hold water, thus representing the element "Water". They can also serve as offering vessels for when you are offering milk, cream, wine, or a spirit to the summoned spirit.

You can spend as little as a dollar at a discount store for this goblet, or spend upwards of $100 on a leaded crystal goblet.

Trust me, the gods won't care one way or the other.

Magick Ink

Some rituals call for special ink, Magick Ink.

You can buy some at a local occult shop, or order off of Amazon, but I tend to make my own.

I have a small bottle of Diamine fountain pen ink I use. I just poke my finger with a diabetic lancet and squeeze a few drops of blood into the ink and BAM! Magick Ink!

You can also go to a hobby store or art store, get a art pen nib and holder, and a bottle of drawing ink.

Same thing – drop a few drops of your blood into it, and it's Magick Ink.

I will use this ink to write my petitions, as well as spells.

When making magick ink, don't use a needle or a razor blade to get blood. We're not after milliliters of your blood, just a few drops. Go find a diabetic lancet, the type used in re-loadable diabetic devices. They're cheap, can be found at any pharmacy in boxes of one hundred. Try to find the larger gauge, like a 26 or 28, as the thinner gauges are easier on your finger, but I have found the thin ones won't allow much blood to appear. You need an actual drop, not a tiny bit needed for blood-glucose meters.

I can't use the auto-poke ones. I'm such a needle-phobic type, hell, I'd die if I ever developed diabetes. I can BARELY poke one of these into a finger.

But – you can BUY magick ink – there are several places, like Amazon that will sell you a bottle. I can't vouch for them, as I make my own.

Parchment Paper (AKA Magick Paper)

There is no need to obtain "magick" paper. In ages past, paper was a rare item, and most magick was written on parchment, usually made from the skins of sheep.

In fact, the name apparently derives from the ancient Greek city of Pergamum (modern Bergama, Turkey), where parchment is said to have been invented in the 2nd century BCE.

In old magick books, you may read that a spell or ritual will need "virgin" parchment. This was because back then, people tended to reuse parchment by scraping the ink from the surface.

For the creation of Sigils and for short petitions, I use a common 4" x 6" scratch pad, easily found at most variety stores. They're usually cheap and I always have several pads on hand.

Once I know the wording of the petition, I'll write it out on the scratch pad, and since it's small, it's easy to burn completely.

Offering Bowl

Unless you are offering wine or spirits, which will be placed into the chalice, most offerings are placed into a special offering bowl.

This can be most anything, from a small woven basket to a small brass bowl with symbols on the sides, which I use myself.

There is really no need to purchase something specifically for this, as any bowl or small plate from your kitchen will work just fine.

Fireproof Bowl

Some rituals will ask that you burn the sigil or petition while working in your circle. For this, you'll obviously need a thick, sturdy bowl, made from pottery, or fired clay. It has to be sturdy enough to allow the paper to burn and not crack and break.

I use a thick soup bowl I purchased at a dollar store.

With this, I recommend a long spoon. I light the paper in a candle flame and then hold it over the bowl, as the paper burns, I will support the paper with the spoon to avoid singeing my fingers.

Two small pie tins, made out of aluminum will also work. Stack them together, to provide a bit of insulation to prevent the altar cloth from being damaged by the heat.

Scrying Mirror

A black scrying mirror can be made quite easily by taking a small non-stick skillet and pouring a small layer of cooking oil in the bottom. The oil's surface, combined with the dark non-stick surface will act as the black mirror.

Many magicians use such a device to help them see the entities that they call upon. For people just beginning, and before your psychic abilities begin to grow, a black mirror is a great way to teach yourself how to see into the invisible dimensions.

Crystal Balls

Another cool item to have around, but I've never been able to get the thing to work for me. Other magicians have used them to see the spirits they've summoned and to get visions of the future.

Me?

Nothing.

Except that they will concentrate a beam of sunlight, like a magnifying glass, and possibly start a fire. So be careful.

Oils!!!

Quite a few people are into essential oils, which helps you to formulate specific magick oils.

You can also buy them already formulated.

Oils are used to "dress" candles. A drop or so in your hand, then rub it on the candle. (For glass-jar candles, use a small screwdriver and jab a hole into the wax, and drop the oil into the hole.)

An oil can be used instead of a traditional incense, but I do recommend the use of real incense if at all possible.

Here's some interesting oil formulas. All the oils start with a base of either almond oil or light mineral oil.

Attract Money:

1/4 cup base oil

To this, add:

- 5 drops Sandalwood
- 5 drops Patchouli
- 2 drops Ginger
- 2 drops Vetivert
- 1 drop Orange

Mix and let it set in a stopupered bottle.

Come to me oil:

1/4 cup base oil

- 2 drops rose geranium
- 2 drops Oil of sweetpea.
- Herbs to add:
- rose petals
- Queen Elizbeth root
- patchouli leaf

Mix, cap in a small bottle and let set a few weeks.

Energy unblock - road opener:

1/4 cup base oil

- Lemon grass oil
- Orange oil
- Dried Abre Camino leaves
- Sage
- Mint
- High John Root

Mix, bottle and let it sit a week.

Abre Camino can be sourced online.

Use this oil to dress a candle with you need to get past any blocks that are causing magick not to manifest.

Misc Items

It's YOUR altar. You can decorate it however you wish.

Many people practicing High Magick will devote their space to a single being, such as Hecate, placing statues and other items associated with the goddess all around their space.

Statues

I personally have statues of Apollo, Aphrodite, Ganesh, and a small angel in bronze I use for Lilith. These small statues can be sourced from local occult shops or Amazon. Be careful when ordering online, as I had ordered a statue of Thoth and received a statue of another being. Then I had to deal with the hassle of making a return.

Mala Beads

These small wooden beads are a nice touch on an altar. I have a set I keep wrapped around a small statue of Ganesh. Looks kinda cool in my bedroom.

Animal Skins

If you're into it, you can also use the fur of animals in and around your altar. I'd avoid using a piece of fur as the altar cloth as candles will drop on the fur and things won't stand very well. Also, of course, make sure the fur is humanely harvested.

Same goes for any antlers, skulls or other bones many use in their altar space.

What you really need

In many ways, I am a minimalist.

I look for ways to streamline any process. So, after years of practicing magick, in all its many forms, I have figured out that most ritualistic magick only needs a few items to make it actually work.

- One candle.
- Offering bowl & Offering
- The God/Goddess image
  - Can be drawn as a sigil
- Your petition

That is really it. Incense is nice but you can use essential oils. Crystals? Not needed. Athame? A figure works just as good. No table? Set up on the floor and sit cross-legged in front of the candle.

The only thing you really need is your intention.

Everything else is icing on the magick cake.

4

Preparation

Determining Your Desire.

Sounds easy enough, right?

Wait. Hold on a second.

It's really not that easy, unless you're a single-minded and determined individual, you may think you know what you want, but is that REALLY what you want?

For example, a lot of people can easily manifest a few bucks now and then, and it's usually easy come, easy go. But what about a reliable monthly income? Building wealth? Finding that perfect soul-mate type person?

Also, the statement of desire should be as simple as possible, and containing enough information to allow the magick to work quickly. Magick, like water or electricity, needs a channel or path for it to flow and be of any use.

Magick must flow.

If you petition a god such as Hermes for an income boost, he'll need some type of path to help you generate income.

Home based businesses and self-employed people know all about opening up income producing channels. But what if you are a slave to the corporation? Then the channels may be limited. Ask for a raise? Maybe. Get that promotion, or apply at another company for a position which has a higher salary? What downsides may exist to those choices?

Being offered a great managerial position at a new company, with a 25% rise in earnings sounds great on paper, what about unpaid overtime? That happens a lot once you get into management!

How about wealth, without having to work too hard? Now, that is something the gods can get their teeth into.

I have been self-employed for decades. It's easy for a god or daemon to get me a flow of money. I'll be hit with an idea, and I'll meditate on the concept, then turn it into a project, either book or online class, or (in the case of my photography) a new paying client who needs multiple photo shoots.

With writing, the month of July 2021 has been my biggest earning month yet with selling books. However, this is the culmination of years of work on my end, with seven books being available. (This book will be my first in the High Magick series).

A lot of books and teachers recommend meditation, but I have found that doesn't work for everyone. The great thing about meditation is that it allows you to get calm and detach.

Because this is how the magick works, the moment you no longer lust after the results, the desire will manifest.

Weird, but true.

It will take some thought as to how to open up new channels, but here's where magick with Gods/Goddesses comes in handy: Ask the God/Goddess for inspiration on what to do to open up channels!

All of my money magick classes include this process.

Thus, you can begin with a ritual to a god to ask for inspiration on how to generate a higher income. Perhaps a ritual involving pendulum work (see appendix) to assist you in narrowing down the choices presented by the Gods.

Thus, when crafting your desire statement, be it wanting a new job, new clients, or love, a soul-mate, whatever it might be, give some thought as to how the desire might come to you!

Onward!

Choosing a Deity

At last look, I saw that there are over 11,000 gods who

have been worshiped at any one time in history. It is my understanding that any god who has ever been worshiped, still exists in some form or another.

That's a lot to choose from.

I tend to work with Grecian deities more than any other group. This is because of my Furies book series, where I did a lot of research into Greek gods and mythologies. I figured they were a pretty interesting bunch (even if Zeus couldn't keep it in his pants).

Apollo, Aphrodite, and Hermes are all subjects of their own books, with a book on Plutus and wealth magick soon to follow. Hecate is a very popular goddess with the wiccans and witches. Many women find the goddess Freya interesting, and work with her. Lilith comes to mind as a good goddess to approach if you wish new and interesting things to appear in your life, or if you have to deal with a business rival, or to see that karma visits someone who has wronged you in ways that left a lasting pain.

Although there are a lot of gods and goddesses that you can choose for magick, the more adventurous practitioner may wish to investigate working with beings other than traditional gods. There is a set of beings known as "Genius Spirits" such as Nitika. Nitika is a great spirit to use for money and wealth, but I'd highly suggest you turn to Hermes or Plutus for your first run at working High Magick.

Maybe you already have an idea of who to call upon. In my class, one student began to see the word "Apollo" almost everywhere she looked. On delivery vans, store signs, a television ad, and more. She asked while in the Q&A of that module, and I straight out told her that Apollo was wanting her to work with him.

There are hundreds, if not thousands, of books about various gods and other beings used in magick. Just don't let the idea of making a choice keep you from working magick. Work with one deity, and see how it goes. You can always summon several Gods, and see whose energy you prefer.

What about Daemons?

The whole point of High Magick, my method, is to make contact with higher beings who are willing and able to help you along your path.

They basically fall into two broad categories: Deities (Gods/Goddess) or Daemons (old country Gods).

Sometimes a specific God/Goddess is now termed a "daemon" but this is mislabeling them and I tend to refer to them as old school Deities. Such as Ba'al, Demiurge, El, Yam, and Astarte.

But, I suggest you work with Deities, as they're more

willing to assist mortals and are more forgiving of students learning. Some daemons can be difficult, so I don't suggest you try calling them forth until you have worked with a few of the other beings that I suggest.

In the past, all deities were dual in nature. They had a "light" side and a "dark" side.

In Hinduism, they have kept the duality of their deities.

Western religions have, essentially, split the gods into two beings.

God (Creator) was split into two, God and Satan (Sometimes Lucifer)

Minor elemental deities became demons.

Many of the deities that High Magick utilize are dualistic in nature.

Wait... How did Gods become Demons?

Gods who became Daemons!

It's not as if one day a particular god woke up to find a letter telling him he was no longer welcome as a God for a particular village, and to pack his bags. It was a process used by the established church to stop pagans from using their well-known gods.

As an example, let's look at the Slavic god Veles.

After the advent of Christianity, Veles was split into

several different characters. As a god of the Underworld and dragons, he, of course, became identified with the Devil. His more benevolent sides were transformed to several Christian saints.

As a protector of cattle, he became associated with Saint Blaise, popularly known among various Slavic nations as St. Vlaho, St. Blaz, or St. Vlasiy.

In Yaroslavl, for example, the first church built on the site of Veles's pagan shrine was dedicated to St Blaise, for the latter's name was similar to Veles and he was likewise considered a heavenly patron of shepherds.

And this is cool: In many Eastern Slavic folk tales, he was replaced by St. Nicholas, probably because the popular stories of the saint describe him as a giver of wealth and a sort of a trickster.

God or Daemon?

Right, so which one?

Allow me to make a few recommendations.

Some Gods who're really open to working with beginners are:

- Hermes: Communication & Business
- Artemis/Diana: Moon Goddess Sacred Feminine, Helps one reach goals, etc.
- Apollo: Health, healing, education, business

opportunities

- Plutus: Wealth and abundance
- Aphrodite/Venus: Love and sex magick
- St. Expedite: a patron saint who helps speed things up.
- Archangel Michael: most anything

Writing Your Desire

Now that you've had some time to think about your desire, it's time to commit it to paper. Don't panic. By working this out on paper, which is step one of writing your petition, you can narrow down what it is you want or need.

Money? Sure, but look at what money can buy.

My mom had been working to manifest a nice house, but she figured it'd come to her via a windfall of money. When she let go of the need for there to be a windfall of money, the house manifested in a different way. My sister and brother-in-law had a parcel of land, 41 acres, and decided to build her a house on this land. My mom picked out the floorplan, the color, and this house was built for her.

By letting go of the HOW, the house manifested.

When writing the desire for a petition, unlike for Law of

Attraction manifestation, or for working a sigil, the desire is written as follows:

"I ask than you bring to me...."

Because you are asking a favor of a god, and if you phrase it as already having happened, then the god will look around, perhaps frown a bit, then shrug and fade away. Why? Well, you might have said "Apollo! I have a large amount of money in the bank!" and he'll be like, "Okay, cool. Why did you call me?"

So, state the desire differently than when you work a sigil.

With your desire formatted, it's easy to reword it for a sigil.

Use a Sigil?

To Sigil or not to Sigil, that is an important question when working magick.

First, what IS a sigil?

A sigil is an abstract representation of your desire, either designed from the letters in your statement of desire or a geometric design using letters converted to numbers. It is used extensively in Chaos magick, and there is a huge number of books, websites and classes over the creation, use, and "firing off" of sigils.

I also incorporate the use of sigils in High Magick, often by adding the name of the god to the sigil as I make one.

The trick to this is to reduce your statement of desire into a manageable sentence so that the sigil itself is easier to draw.

For example, this sigil is comprised of a single short sentence: "I have a million dollars"

This is just using the letters "HVMLNDRS " which are all that are left after removing all vowels and duplicated consonants.

Then I converted the letters into numbers, and overlayed them on a planetary square of Jupiter. Which gives me this:

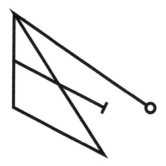

There is a complete set of directions on sigil creation in the Appendix and in the companion workbook.

Offerings

What do you give to a God/Goddess who has everything?

Allow me to make a couple of suggestions. And if you consult the Google Mystery School, you'll get thousands of results and then have to wade through them, when the correct answer is usually: ASK.

If you happen to have any talent as a medium or psychic, you can reach out using a simplified ritual and just ask Hermes, or Apollo, or Plutus what they'd like to have as an offering. Use the "Brief Ritual" as outlined later in this book.

Allow me to suggest the follow as suitable offerings acceptable by most of the gods I'm suggesting:

- Flowers
- Incense
- Small shot of liquor/wine
- Milk or cream
- Honey (Organic)
- Fruit (fresh, organic)
- Fresh herbs
- An item suggested by the deity

Make sure to have a container for the offering. If liquid, pour the wine/spirit/milk/etc into a holding container and then, at the appropriate time in the ritual, hand over the offering. I use a small brass bowl for this.

After about 24 hrs, or a week (but keep an eye on any liquids as they'll begin to mold or evaporate and leave disgusting messes behind) remove the offering and take it outside.

Timing for your Ritual

This is the nice part about doing this type of High Magick, is that it really doesn't matter when you work the ritual.

However, the energies that exist around specific days of the week and moon phases can lend some assistance to your power.

What I list below are summaries of the magick correspondences for specific times and moon phases. This list is by no means complete.

Days of the week:

Sunday = The day of the Sun. Useful for healing, creativity, success.

Monday = The day of the Moon (Hecate). Travel, fertility,

farming, psychic powers.

Tuesday = The day of Mars (Ares). Overcoming challenges, cursing others, psychic attack.

Wednesday = The day of Mercury (Hermes). Magick that needs communication,

Thursday = The day of Jupiter (Zeus). Business, money, wealth, abundance.

Friday = The day of Venus (Aphrodite). Love and family rituals work best this day.

Saturday = The day of Saturn. Banishing, karma retribution, protection, curse breaking.

Moon Phases:

New Moon = Restarts. Work magick intended to bring to you anything.

New Moon to Full Moon (Waxing Moon) = Magick to start a business, garden, romance. Think of this period as the "Bring to me" phase.

Full Moon= Major magick time. Working with a moon goddess (Hecate) at this point in time. Energy builds as the moon grows full, and timing for this is anywhere from two days before the full moon to one day after full moon.

Full Moon towards New Moon (Waning Moon). Magick to release things. Magick to break curses, remove blocks, remove toxic people.

Time of Day

There is quite a bit written about using specific times of the day for magick.

The hours after sun rise until sun set are divided and assigned to various planets. The hours after sun set until sun rise are also divided and assigned to planets. There are websites which will assist you in the calculations for this, as the times of the planets vary during the week as well your location. I recommend a website to help you calculate this, such as astrology.com.

Thus, you can work a business ritual on a Thursday during the hour of Jupiter, after the new moon.

5

The High Magick Ritual

The typical high Magick ritual I work is outlined as follows.

The Petition

A petition is like a spell, in which you are requesting aid from a deity or higher being.

Far more powerful than the usual pre-written spell. You craft your petition once you know your desire, and it can be combined with making a sigil. Take your time, make several drafts. Then, using the magick ink, write your petition.

On the night of your ritual, bring the ink and pen with you into the circle, along with the prepared petition.

After the opening evocation to bring forth the entity you wish to petition, you then read the petition aloud, sign it with the magick ink, and if you're crafting a sigil, draw it and have it ready for the ritual.

Also, you should burn the petition in the fire-proof bowl.

The basic petition is usually formatted as follows:

- Praise to God/Goddess

- Your desire

- How you wish it to come

- What you're offering in return

- Express gratitude for the God/Goddess granting your petition.

Then sign it. You might want to meditate over it, then light it with a candle, allow the paper to burn to ash while in the ritual.

Later, take the ash into nature (backyard, park, where-ever) and discard it.

Sample Petition:

This is simply how I write a petition to a god, such as Apollo. You can word yours similarly, or place everything into your own words.

(Deity's name) I ask that you come forward, grace me with your presence.

I ask that you, (Deity's Name) join me now.

I seek your advice,

I seek your knowledge,

I seek your company.

I ask that (insert your desire)

I ask that this be delivered swiftly in a manner that is safe for all concerned.

I am ready to receive your bounty, grant me this desire,

It is a desire I hold in the very core of my being.

Please accept my humble offering to you, oh (Deity's Name)

In return for granting me this desire, I shall:

(What you plan to give, offer)

I thank you, oh (Deity's Name) for your company,

I thank you for this boon,

I offer my sincerest gratitude to you for granting me my desire.

Once written, put it in a safe place until time for your ritual.

OPTIONAL: You may also place the Deity's Seal at the top, and craft a sigil at the bottom.

Invocation vs evocation

Briefly, an evocation is calling upon the spirit to drop by, like inviting a friend over for holiday dinner.

Invocation, on the other hand, is like a Jury Duty summons. Come over right this second, or I'll banish you into the netherworld, blah blah... So, don't be surprised if the being shows up in a grumpy mood and accepts your petition but never acts upon it.

Therefore, in this book, I only instruct in the use of evocation. Unless you're dealing with a being who's more of an Angelic, who needs some words of power uttered to get their cooperation. I'll go over this in the chapter on Angelic High Magick.

The High Magick Ritual

As Beetlejuice said, "It's SHOW-TIME!"

Take a few deep breaths, in and out, slowly.

Quiet your mind.

Add some incense to the burner, make sure all tools are handy, and either sit, or kneel, or stand. I prefer sitting because I get a bit wobbly as I meditate while standing. Kneeling can also work, but with my knees, I'll sit, thank you!

Step One: Casting The Circle

With my type of magick, a circle is used less for *protection,* and more for opening up a channel through which you make contact with the energy of the universe and the particular god you wish to summon.

If you work in an area known for negativity, or you have a temporary space, this circle will also allow you to sanctify the space and eject any negative energies.

If this is the case, and you are just beginning, I then suggest using the banishing ritual while casting your circle. I'll cover both in this chapter.

Make sure you have space to walk all around your table/altar.

Get the incense going, and all ritual candles are lit (save the one candle for your desire).

Make sure to mark the directions, as you start with facing north in this method and then walk CLOCK-wise around your altar.

As you walk, aim the athame, crystal point or a finger at the ground, defining the circle.

In your mind, imagine golden light, like a laser or liquid sunlight, shooting out of the pointing device, and leaving a visible trail in the floor.

When you get to the starting point, stop and face north.

In your mind, see the circle of light on the floor expand

and flow upwards, creating a cylinder which goes up into the space above you, creating a pillar of energy. Make sure to see this fully in your mind.

Say: "I have now cast this circle. I now banish all non-positive energies from this space!"

Sweep in a circle and, when facing WEST, act as if you are tossing away the negative energies.

Another method is as follows, which you can add onto the circle casting above:

Purification:

Be silent and see the gold light expanding around you, out-wards to the edges of the circle you just cast.

It fills the entire space with bright, golden light.

Say:

I purify my BODY of all sickness, disease, illness, and toxins.

May it be healthy and strong, healed and whole - a proper temple for the expression of my spirit!

I purify my MIND of all stray thoughts, so that it may be as crisp and clear as a mountain zephyr.

May it be receptive to divine guidance, and learn to discern truth from lie. May it be insightful, inspired, and motivated!

I purify my WILL. May it remain strong and steadfast when it has set upon the path of the greater good.

May it never waver, but give me the courage to fulfill my destiny to the best of my capabilities and the fullest of my potential!

I purify my EMOTIONS. May they flow as as freely as a rushing woodland stream.

May they never stagnate, but express themselves in constructive ways. Help me in matters of joy and intuition

***

Another method, which uses a summoning of beings from each direction, and this particular circle casting is widely used by people who following the Wiccan way of ritual. Some people may find this more appealing than the previous method.

1. Place four (4) makers to represent north, south, east and west. (These can be anything, even pencils for the witch in hiding.)

2. Stand in the center of the circle and say:

I cast this circle to enhance my energies and to protect me from all harm. I cast this circle and only the most balanced and positive energies may enter.

3. Now the caster is to call upon the elements:

I call upon the guardians and the watchtowers of the north/east/south/west elements of earth/air/fire/water. Guard and guide me. Hail and welcome.

4. Now call on the Lord and Lady by saying:

I call upon the Lord and Lady and the Great Spirit to lend their energies and protect me.

5. When done say:

My work is done, Thank you elements of earth, air, fire and water; Great Spirit and Lord and Lady, may my magic disperse into the universe and may my circle end.

That's pretty much it for casting your circle. Don't get too caught up in what needs to be said, as long as you hold your intent on the task at hand and establishing a channel of communication for your work.

Copy this down by hand so you can have it handy when in your space for a ritual.

Step Two(ish) Time to get to work: Calling the Deity

Now, the Invocation:

Address the being using any salutation you feel is appropriate.

I'll often simply state:

I ask that you come forward, grace me with your presence.

I ask that you, (Deity's Name) join me now.

I seek your advice,

I seek your knowledge,

I seek your company.

Another possible way of invoking the god is as follows:

God/Goddess of the (Planet, Day, Etc), You have been known by many names in many lands in many times.

You are universal and constant. In the dark of night, You shine down upon me and bathe me in Your light and love.

I ask You, O Divine One, to honor me by joining with me, and allowing me to feel Your presence within my heart.

The gods will respond as long as you do this while in a calm state of mind, and say this with sincere desire for the god to manifest with you in the circle.

At this point, pause a few heartbeats, then proceed.

Step Three: Presenting the petition

This is where you take your prepared Sigil and Petition in hand.

Face north.

Go into a light Alpha state of mind. Visualize what is it you wish to have happen. Run a mental movie of this happening. Make it as real as possible.

When ready, and feeling the presence of the divine near you, recite your petition.

After reciting your petition, pause a moment, then ask: "Will you grant me this (petition/request)?"

If you hear "Yes"… then sign your name with the magick ink at the bottom of the petition.

Then, carefully, light the edge of the paper and allow it to burn to ash in the fireproof bowl. You can stir the ashes with the spoon to make sure the petition completely reduced to ash.

Step Four: Offering

At this point in the ritual, it's time to hand over the offering.

My best advice here is to use a statement similar to this one:

"Oh (Being's Name) please accept this humble offering as a gift for acting upon my petition in a timely manner."

At this point, pour any liquid into the offering bowl, or if using a solid item (flowers) place these on the symbol of the being you've just petitioned.

Step Five: Communion with the Spirit/God/Goddess and Dismissal

Sit quietly, and breath in a rhythmic pattern.

If you wish to use a black scrying mirror, place it in your field of vision now.

Allow yourself to enter into a light trance state.

Ask your guest if they have any advice for you with regards to the petition/sigil.

Stay quiet. Listen.

Know this: **The Deity/Angel/Demon speaks to you through your thoughts via telepathy. With telepathy, the words of the Being come to you through your thoughts. In** the beginning, it can be difficult for those who are not as sensitive or lack psychic ability to differentiate between the communication from another entity and their own thoughts. With proper meditation and experience, this becomes much easier over time.

Once about a minute has passed, thank the entity for their presence in this ritual, and thank them for their assistance, and allow them to leave, if they wish.

Proper dismissal is as follows:

"I thank you for your attention to my petition. As you came in peace, please depart in peace, come again when I next call upon you."

Give thanks to the universe for allowing the petition to be answered or sigil to manifest.

A Summary of the Ritual

The basic steps for a basic High Magick ritual

1. **Choose a Being to Summon**

2. **Prepare your petition**

3. **Decide on an offering**

4. **Prepare your space and cast the circle**

5. **Purify the space with a banishing**

6. **Invoke the Being**

7. **Present the Petition**

8. **Meditate on the outcome**

9. **Give over the offering**

10. **Communion (more meditation)**

11. **Close the ritual.**

Magick simply opens the doors, it is up to you to implement the physical actions that will be needed to fully manifest your desires.

Be alert for any whispers near you that contain guidance on what you need to do. Often, it's a gentle nudge, but sometimes it's a shout in your ear!

6

The Saints and High Magick

Yes, you can work with Saints.

That's the answer to a lot of questions I get in my email I was giving these classes. People with a background in traditional faiths would often ask if there is a way to work with beings they already know, versus the usual deities often associated with High Magick.

There are over 10,000 Saints in the Catholic tradition. Some, like Saint Expedite, have crossed over into the areas of HooDoo, Cajun Magick, Swamp magick, etc.

In High Magick, we tend to look at Saints as minor deities. There are two basic ways to work with a Saint, one is with the use of Novenas and prayers.

I call this the "Right Hand Path". Here, you kneel in prayer and bow, pledging fealty to that god, or Saint.

The other, used by magicians who are on the Left-Hand path, use a more typical evocation to bring the Saint into our presence. Then we literally command the spirit to do our bidding.

In the Left Hand, we also take full responsibility for our successes and failures with Magick, we do not lay the blame at the feet of the spirit, but we do thank the spirits for their help.

Actually, this gets better results than Novenas, unless you have a traditional upbringing that venerated Saints, in which case it'll probably work fine.

Because magick is all based upon your core beliefs, one way might work better for you than another.

I shall present BOTH ways of working with the Saints. I will lay out the traditional novena prayers to Saint Expedite and Saint Michael, and an evocation of Saint Expedite using the same calls I use for invoking/evoking Angels.

First up, let's take a look at Saint Expedite, an unusual Saint and one I became acquainted with only last year.

One of the more unique Saints in the Roman Catholic tradition, Saint Expedite is known for delivering on your prayers quickly.

His history is either based upon a real Roman soldier who

lived in the 3rd Century, or is a case of mistaken identity caused by a crate of statues arriving at a cathedral, with the word "Expedite" on the side.

The nuns figured this was the name of the Saint whose statue was in the box.

Either way, this Saint is known to deliver on your prayers in a rapid manner. Sometimes within 48 hours.

I have read several origin stories, but the fact remains, this Saint is revered all across Europe and in the southern United States, most notably in New Orleans.

Multiple websites exist which focus on this Saint, and they all seem to agree on the prayers and offerings to Saint Expedite.

Taking the Right-Hand path, one of the requirements of petitioning Saint Expedite is to publicly thank him for answering your prayers. There are a few pages and groups on Facebook, and there are a few websites for this as well.

As with other novenas to Saints, the outcome is based upon the faith that the petitioner has that the saint will perform the miracles that is requested.

The novenas that follow are traditional prayers to Saint Expedite. They are found in multiple books and several websites and are presented here as found.

What you will need:

- Image or statue of the saint

- Red Candle, the tall novena 7-day candle

- A glass of water

- An offering

- Pound Cake (or other sweet bread/cake)

- Roses

- Red Wine

Then a space for the altar and a LOT of time.

Ritual to Saint Expedite

The set-up is simple.

Image of Saint Expedite at the back of the altar. The red candle on the right, and the glass of water on the left. The water is used for the flowers.

Typically, one lights the candle then says one of the many prayers.

I also go on and do a small offering of wine or cake at that time. A taste of what he'll get when he delivers. (Essentially, a bribe)

The following is a sample "novena" to Saint Expedite

Prayer to Saint Expedite (#1)

Saint Expedite, you lay in rest.

I come to you and ask that

this wish be granted.

   (your wish)

Expedite now what I ask of you.

Expedite now what I want of you,

 this very second.

Don't waste another day.

Give me what I ask for.

I know your power,

I know you because of your work.

I know you can do it.

Do this for me and I'll

(your offering)

Expedite this wish with speed,

honor, and goodness.

Glory to you, Saint Expedite!

Okay, got all that? Now repeat for at least nine straight days. That's what "novena" essentially means, 9-days. But, no… Not this method.

This method requires you to continually say the prayer,

and keep a red candle burning, until your wish is granted.

Personally, I went through FOUR candles until I finally invoked him using the left hand path.

Direct Evocation of Saint Expedite

CAUTION: This uses the sacred names of God to bind and bring the Saint to you. It's like when a court subpoenas you and they send a cop to drag you to the court.

This needs the image or statue.

Only one candle. Go with a color that represents your desire (or white, it's good for most anything)

Notice that there is no offering. Why? Look. If you have to drag this guy to you, why offer anything?

Opening chant (3x)

EE-AH-OH-EH (Yahweh in original Hebrew)

Meditate on what is needed, the saint helping.

EE-AH-OH-EH (3x)

SAINT EXPEDITE (3x)

In the names of

ELL, ELL-OH-HEEM ADD-OH-NIGH, ADD-EAR-EAR-ORN

EH-EE-EH ASHER EH-EE-EH

EL SHAD-EYE

I call on thee SAINT EXPEDITE

I call thee, SAINT EXPEDITE, by the power of

AH-KAH-TREE-ELL

EE-AH-OH-EH-TZAH-VAH-OAT

Hear my call SAINT EXPEDITE and know that I

ask

Now, tell him what you want him to bring to you. Be brief. Then…

HA-EE-YAH (3X) See the old situation

HAW-YEAH (3X) See the Angel helping

YEE-YAH (3X) See the result.

GO IN PEACE SAINT EXPEDITE

I must note, this made the fellow appear. Part of my request was that he shows up to my mother and at least listen to her request.

That evening, my mother reported an odd glowing light in her office then in her basement, which appeared after the basement door opened and then shut.

Angelic Magick

This section will be fairly brief. In the previous chapter I introduced the concept of evocation of Saints and now we'll look at using this method to call on "Angelic" beings, specifically Saint Michael.

Saint Michael is also known as Archangel Michael.

On some websites, there are illustrations of him in a full suit of armor. It is interesting to note than when I did a calling to him as Archangel, that is how he showed himself to me.

Various sources document that Saint Michael is a good one to have in your corner when to comes to business and finance. He's also quite good for protection.

I'll start with the usual Novenas prayed to Saint Michael. As you can see, you subjugate yourself to their God, giving over your destiny in the hopes the guy will grant your prayer.

I have invoked him as an Archangel, and he will come when he is summoned using the Left-Hand path.

Summoning him using the Left-Hand path, he appeared looking a LOT like his statues.

He towered over me, then rammed his sword into the garage floor.

It left a rather deep broken area in the floor.

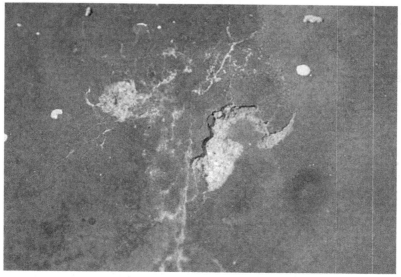

(Not sure if this will show up decently on Kindle.. On a tablet it looks nice!)

Here's the usual Right Hand Path ritual to summon Archangel Michael (or any of the others)

With the Right-Hand Path – expect to say a Novena at least NINE times. With some Saints, the Novena changes from day to day. Thus, there will be nine novenas said over the course of nine days.

Now you can see why the Left-Hand Path is a bit more useful for those of us who prefer to be in charge.

Like with Saint Expedite, you'll need a space set up for this.

An image or statue of the Saint.

A novena type candle with his image on it (spotted in most

stores in religious neighborhoods)

An offering. Flowers. Honey. Promising fealty to the Christian Gods.

This novena is to be repeated every day for at least nine days:

St. Michael the Archangel, we honor you as a powerful protector of the Church and guardian of our souls.

Inspire us with your humility, courage, and strength that we may reject sin and perfect our love for our Heavenly Father.

In your strength and humility, slay the evil and pride in our hearts so that nothing will keep us from God. St. Michael the Archangel, pray that we may be blessed by God with the zeal to live our lives in accordance with Christ's teachings.

St. Michael the Archangel, you are the prince of angels but in your humility, you recognized that God is God and you are but His servant.

Unlike Satan, you were not overcome with pride but were steadfast in humility.

Pray that we will have this same humility.

It is in the spirit of that humility that we ask for your intercession for our petitions... (state your petitions)

Saint Michael the Archangel, defend us in battle, be our protection against the wickedness and snares of the devil.

May God rebuke him, we humbly pray; and do thou, O Prince of the Heavenly host, by the power of God, thrust into hell Satan and all the evil spirits who prowl about the world seeking the ruin of souls."

In the name of the Father, and of the Son, and of the Holy Spirit. Amen

Got that? Do this nine days and he might, just maybe, show up and grant you your desire.

***

Now, let's look at the Left Hand Path method.

For this, locate a simple line drawing of Archangel Michael (One provided in the back of the book)

The Left-Hand path can be like the one for Saint Expedite, which is as follows (this is in your handout):

Ritual to Michael

Opening chant (3x)

EE-AH-OH-EH

Meditate on what is needed, the angel helping.

Chat 3 x

EE-AH-OH-EH

Look at the image of Archangel Micheal

Call to the angel

MEEK-AH-ELL (3x)

Main Calling.

Say:

> *In the names of*
>
> *ELL, ELL-OH-HEEM ADD-OH-NIGH,*

ADD-EAR-EAR-ORN

> *EH-EE-EH ASHER EH-EE-EH*
>
> *EL SHAD-EYE*
>
> *I call on thee MEEK-AH-ELL*
>
> *I call thee, MEEK-AH-ELL, by the power of*
>
> *AH-KAH-TREE-ELL*
>
> *EE-AH-OH-EH-TZAH-VAH-OAT*
>
> *Hear my call MEEK-AH-ELL and know that*

I ask

State your request

Look at his image again.

Then Chant

> *HA-EE-YAH (3X) See the old situation*
>
> *HAW-YEAH (3X) See the Angel helping*
>
> *YEE-YAH (3X) See the result.*
>
> *GO IN PEACE MEEK-AH-ELL*

That's it! You're done!

7

Troubleshooting Magick

When will this all begin to work?

What should I expect?

When should I work another ritual?

Honestly, I see these questions in many magick groups and in my email.

Part of this entire process is to hand over the magick manifestation of your desire to a non-physical cosmic being, who's main task is to rearrange reality to allow you to realize your desire.

This is the non-physical part. This is the universe working to rearrange the "quantum" state to collapse and allow your desire to manifest.

You are in charge of the physical part.

Some of this is taking physical action which will assist the magick.

The physical action might be to sit quiet, listen for advice whispered into your mind, then write a business plan to open a new business, write some ads which will bring you clients, or a feeling of being pushed to attend an opening of a new library, where you will run into someone new and exciting who is also being pushed to meet you.

Your mental reactions to our physical reality has more to do with how things manifest than any other aspect of magick. If you begin to question the *HOW*, how will the magick manifest, you've already taken five steps back.

Mindset

Another part of the magick is your mindset.

Many, many books go into detail on how to control your expectations about magick, how to disconnect from the outcome, how not to "Lust For Results". By simply asking those questions, you will work to shift the energy just enough you miss the inspiration for the physical steps you need to take to make a shift in your reality.

If you are working money magick, it's the checking of your bank account and that upwelling of panic when the balance stays in the single digits. It the panic that rises up when your email is empty, instead of being filled with orders and new contacts.

As this goes on, you might begin to ignore the subtle signs your magick is about to work. With money magick, you might actually receive a small sum, and then you react like "Is this all?"

That reaction can grind the magick to a halt.

But, sometimes, there can be an outside force that causes your magick to slow down, or even totally fail.

Outside forces

What are these outside forces?

It can be as simple as someone in your circle who is projecting, either consciousness or unconsciously, the energy of doubt.

This energy can be very powerful, and can affect your own magick energy.

This is why I caution people to keep their rituals secret. But we love to talk about our work, and this is especially true in groups where people often share their magick efforts.

The doubt can be from anyone, not just people who might be jealous of your success. People who carry a strong energy of doubt, disbelievers, can project such doubt, it'll have a negating effect on any magick you might be working.

These blocks can manifest as pretty much anything. Communications issues, such as marketing emails bouncing, Facebook limitations suddenly being imposed on you, deposits on hold by your bank.

Fathoming out external blocks takes a bit more detective work.

So, I generally suggest block removal magick, and road opener magick.

Block Removal

Internal blocks will respond well to a general road opener spell. External blocks will respond as well, but possibly not as intended.

Road Opener

A general road-opener spell can be done in many, many differing ways.

The classic spell needs some candles, Road Opener oil that contains the special herb, abre camino, which can be sourced from most magick herbal shops. (See my recipe from the chapter on Tools)

If you can get this, then it's a simple matter of drying the herb, coating an orange candle with it, and burning it. Then go and bury the wax puddle by a road or at a cross-roads, preferably a dirt road.

I will coat the candle in light oil, almond or olive oil, roll the candle in the crushed and powdered herb, then set the candle in a sturdy holder that'll allow the candle to burn and leave some wax. A thick pillar candle dish works well, or two aluminum pie tins set on each other.

Project your intention into the candle, seeing the roads suddenly opening up, then light the candle. Burn safely, keeping it away from anything that can catch fire. Allow it to burn completely.

You can also use a "block removal" oil and coat an orange candle with it, and it typically works just as well.

Purchasing a "Road Opener" candle from a reliable source can also be done, just remember to place your intention firmly into the candle.

Jar Spells can also work.

You can find these items, possibly at magick shops. I am lucky to have most of this in the woods nearby.

- Pine Needles
- Sea Salt
- Coffee beans
- Rose petals
- Lavender

• Small jar

Combine a small amount of each item into a single small jar. Place your intention into this jar, and then go bury it in a garden. Burying in the earth will begin to use "earth" energy in removing most blocks.

Petition a God or Goddess

Rule one - never blame a god for magick not working.

Using a pendulum and a spirit board, make contact with the god you summoned, and see if you can get answers as to what is blocking you. Use tarot if the pendulum won't work, or if you prefer to use the tarot.

Then summon a being to you and ask for them to act by making a petition to remove any blocks or energy aimed at you. Use the ritual system in this book, and make your intention clear to remove all blocks, both internal and external, blocks placed by unknowing people and blocks placed on purpose.

Final Thoughts

Okay, you've made it this far, which is good. There're no random gods wandering your house, eating all the candy, and scaring your cat.

Magick can be very, very effective. The entire key to making it work isn't trying new rituals if the first one fails to work, but figuring out what you did wrong in the first place.

I had a dismal success rate at first. I felt I was damned lucky when it'd work the first time out, and I tended to do what I call "Kitchen Sink" magick: I'd throw everything – except the kitchen sink – at a problem until the problem was resolved.

Instead, look at each problem you want solved by magick as a project in science. Change one thing at a time and look at the results. This also includes making a log of your rituals and keeping track of what you did and how the ritual is working out.

The companion workbook has premade pages to assist you in keeping a log of the details of your rituals, the time, the deity, and the offering.

Work one program or goal at a time. When you first begin, working multiple rituals for separate goals can scatter your energy and might keep any magick from working.

Start small, or pursue modest goals, and feel the success of the magick, which will lead you to bigger and better magick.

That's it for High Magick 101! Good luck and may the grace of the gods be with you!

Appendix

Links:

Planetary time calculator:

>   https://www.astrology.com.tr/planetary-hours.asp

Source for Abre Camino:

>   https://www.originalbotanica.com

Complex Sigils Creation

Some people will try to convince you that sigil creation is some type of complicated process and is all occult and ultra-top secret.

The information is all out there (meaning the interwebs) so what I am about to show you here isn't new, isn't some wild idea of my own, it's been used for well over 125 years. (Like the term "magick" or "magik", sheesh!)

Once you have a summary of your desire, phrased as a "past tense" statement, you will have a sentence of about 5 to 10 words.

Past tense simply means you phrase a desire as if it has already occurred.

A statement such as "I have one million dollars" would be a good example.

A statement such as "I wish to receive a huge sum of money" isn't. It's in future tense, uses a soft way of asking, "wish" and the money isn't well defined.

Forget about HOW the money will come to you, you already have it.

So, taking this statement, you'd look at what letters exist, then cross out each vowel (and I include the vowel "y" in this).

Thus, the following happens:

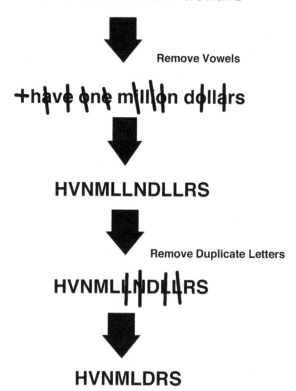

I have one million dollars

Remove Vowels

HVNMLLNDLLRS

Remove Duplicate Letters

HVNMLDRS

Here's the resulting sigil created with those letters:

Nothing fancy, just a design using the letters. I whipped this up in Photoshop, but drawing this by hand is much more effective.

To take this further, you convert the letters to numbers, using any one of a number of translation methods. Once you have the letters converted, you map the numbers on a planetary square to generate a sigil based upon the magick of that planet!

My favorite is the use of the "Jewish Gematria":

Jewish Gematria

A=1	J=600	S=90
B=2	K=10	T=100
C=3	L=20	U=200
D=4	M=30	V=700
E=5	N=40	W=900
F=6	O=50	X=300
G=7	P=60	Y=400
H=8	Q=70	Z=500
I=9	R=80	

Thus, the letters "HVNMLDRS" will become

8, 700, 40, 30, 20, 4, 80, 90

If you look at the magick square of Jupiter, it only goes from 1-12, so you have to reduce the numbers to their lowest logical number. Thus, 700 becomes 7.

Now, we have 8,7,4,3,2,8,9

Overlay this on the Jupiter square:

4	14	15	1
9	7	6	12
5	11	10	8
16	2	3	13

Draw a large dot over the letter 8, then a line to the rest of the numbers in order as shown.

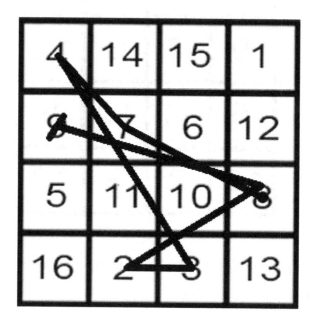

Then take the square away and you have the "working magic sigil"

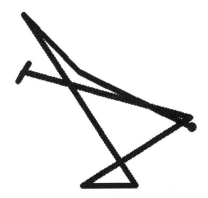

The various planetary squares are at the end of the book, after the table of correspondences.

The Pendulum and Magick

Many of us already have a pendulum. It was one of the first tools I acquired a long time ago. I still use mine, mostly for divination.

But it can be used to contact spirit when worked with a letter circle. I have included an old pendulum dowsing chart I found in the pre-Internet days.

The pendulum is only as accurate as your own intuition, but I have a small secret to share, a way to increase your accuracy with the pendulum

Using "Programmed" water, you can greatly increase your accuracy with ANY divination method.

Programmed water is a technique pioneered by Dr Masaru Emoto. I'm not going to go into the history of his research, that's easily found on what we call the "Google Mystery School".

Instead, I'll show you how to use it to increase accuracy with working with the pendulum.

You will need a small water bottle (I use an old Gatorade bottle)

A piece of paper

A marker

Tape

Patience

Write a term like "Truth" or "only the truth" on the paper

Tape it to the bottle

Let it sit for at least 72 hours.

Then, when ready for a pendulum session, take a few sips of this water to activate that suggestion, and allow the water to diffuse into your body.

Planetary Squares:

THE *KAMEA* OF THE SUN
& PLANETARY SIGILS

6	32	3	34	35	1
7	11	27	28	8	30
19	14	16	15	23	24
18	20	22	21	17	13
25	29	10	9	26	12
36	5	33	4	2	31

- Each row and column contains six numbers.
- The square contains 36 numbers from 1 to 36.
- Each row, column and diagonal adds up to 111.
- All of the numbers in the square add up to 666.

THE *KAMEA* OF MERCURY
& PLANETARY SIGILS

8	58	59	5	4	62	63	1
49	15	14	52	53	11	10	56
41	23	22	44	45	19	18	48
32	34	35	29	28	38	39	25
40	26	27	37	36	30	31	33
17	47	46	20	21	43	42	24
9	55	54	12	13	51	50	16
64	2	3	61	60	6	7	57

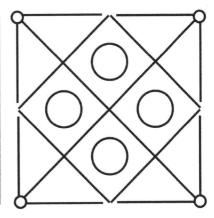

* Each row and column contains eight numbers
* The square contains 64 numbers from 1 to 64
* Each row, column and diagonal adds up to 260.
* All of the numbers in the square add up to 2080

David Thompson

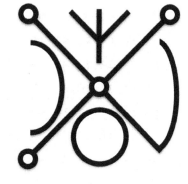

**THE *KAMEA* OF VENUS
& PLANETARY SIGILS**

22	47	16	41	10	35	4
5	23	48	17	42	11	29
30	6	24	49	18	36	12
13	31	7	25	43	19	37
38	14	32	1	26	44	20
21	39	8	33	2	27	45
46	15	40	9	34	3	28

• Each row and column contains seven numbers
• The square contains 49 numbers from 1 to 49
• Each row, column and diagonal adds up to 175.
• All of the numbers in the square add up to 1225

THE *KAMEA* OF LUNA
& PLANETARY SIGILS

37	78	29	70	21	62	13	54	5
6	38	79	30	71	22	63	14	46
47	7	39	80	31	72	23	55	15
16	48	8	40	81	32	64	24	56
57	17	49	9	41	73	33	65	25
26	58	18	50	1	42	74	34	66
67	27	59	10	51	2	43	75	35
36	68	19	60	11	52	3	44	76
77	28	69	20	61	12	53	4	45

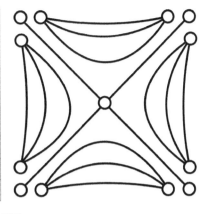

- Each row and column contains nine numbers
- The square contains 81 numbers from 1 to 81
- Each row, column and diagonal adds up to 260.
- All of the numbers in the square add up to 2080

THE KAMEA AND SIGIL OF MARS

11	24	7	20	3
4	12	25	8	16
17	5	13	21	9
10	18	1	14	22
23	6	19	2	15

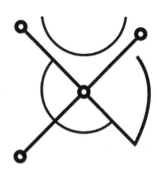

The Sigils or Seals of Mars

The *Kamea*, or Magic Square, of Mars, has the numbers 5, 25, 65, and 325 as its keys:
- Each row, column and diagonal has 5 squares.
- There are 25 boxes, holding 1 through 25
- Each row, column and diagonal adds to 65
- All the numbers add to 325

THE *KAMEA* OF JUPITER
& PLANETARY SIGILS

4	14	15	1
9	7	6	12
5	11	10	8
16	2	3	13

- Each row and column contains 4 numbers
- The square contains 16 numbers from 1 to 16
- Each row, column and diagonal adds up to 34.
- All of the numbers in the square add up to 136

The *Kamea* and Seal and Sign of Saturn

4	9	2
3	5	7
8	1	6

ד	ט	ב
ג	ה	ז
ח	א	ו

- Each row and column contains three numbers
- The square contains 9 numbers from 1 to 9
- Each row, column and diagonal adds up to 15.
- All of the numbers in the square add up to 45

Correspondences

Here are the meanings of different candle colors in general:

• White candles -Destruction of negative energy, peace, truth, and purity

• Purple candles- Spiritual awareness, wisdom, tranquility

• Lavender Candles– Intuition, Paranormal, Peace, Healing

• Blue and Deep Blue Candles– Meditation, Healing, Forgiveness, Inspiration, Fidelity, Happiness, and opening lines of Communication.

• Green Candles– Money, Fertility, Luck, Abundance, Health (not to be used when diagnosed with Cancer), Success

• Rose and Pink Colored Candles– Positive self-love, friendship, harmony, joy

• Yellow Candles- Realizing and manifesting thoughts, opening up communication, confidence, bringing plans into action, creativity, intelligence, mental clarity, clairvoyance.

• Orange Candles– Joy, energy, education, strength attraction, stimulation

• Red or Deep red Candles– Passion, energy, love, lust, relationships, sex, vitality, courage.

• Black Candles– Protection, absorption and destruction of negative energy and also repelling negative energy from others

• Silver candle– Goddess or feminine energy, remove negativity, psychic development, money

• Gold candle– Male energy, Solar energy, fortune, spiritual attainment, money.

Candle colors and Days:

- Sunday– Gold or yellow candles
- Monday– Silver, Grey or White
- Tuesday-Red
- Wednesday-Purple
- Thursday– Blue
- Friday-Green
- Saturday– Black or Purple

Candle colors and healing purposes:

- Allergies- Violet
- Anxiety- Rose
- Colds- Green/violet
- Depression-Orange/Indigo/Rose
- Insomnia-Blue
- Indigestion-Yellow
- Fever-Blue
- Headaches-Green/blue
- Diabetes-Yellow

White

- The Goddess
- Higher Self
- Purity
- Peace
- Virginity
- (substitutes any other color)

Black

- Binding
- Shapeshifting
- Protection
- Repels Negativity

Brown

- Special Favors
- To Influence Friendships

Silver

- The Goddess
- Astral energy
- Female energy
- Telepathy
- Clairvoyance
- Intuition
- Dreams

Purple

- Third Eye
- Psychic Ability
- Hidden Knowledge
- To Influence People in High Places
- Spiritual Power

Blue

- Element of Water

- Wisdom
- Protection
- Calm
- Good Fortune
- Opening Blocked Communication
- Spiritual Inspiration

Green

- The Element of Earth
- Physical Healing
- Monetary success
- Mother Earth
- Tree and Plant Magic
- Growth
- Personal Goals

Pink

- Affection
- Romance
- Affection
- Caring
- Nurturing
- Planetary Good Will

Red

- Element of Fire
- Passion
- Strength
- Fast action

- Career Goals
- Lust
- Driving Force
- Survival
- Blood of the Moon

Orange

- General Success
- Property Deals
- Legal matters
- Justice
- Selling

Copper

- Professional Growth
- Business Fertility
- Career Maneuvers
- Passion
- Money Goals

Gold

- The God
- Promote Winning
- Power of the Male
- Happiness

Yellow

- The Element of Air
- Intelligence

- The Sun
- Memory
- Logical Imagination
- To Accelerate Learning
- To Break Mental Blocks

Archangel Michael illustration

David Thompson

Other Magick Books by David Thompson:

Grecian Magick Series (Apollo, Aphrodite, Hermes)

https://www.amazon.com/gp/product/B0968WVKHW

Dave's Facebook Page:

https://www.facebook.com/DavePsychic/

Secrets of Magick Facebook Group:

https://www.facebook.com/groups/secretsofmagick

And finally, Dave's webpage, book readings and his services:

https://davepsychic.com

Made in the USA
Middletown, DE
13 October 2023

40736422R00060